Be Prepared

A Book on Terrorism Awareness and

Emergency Response

By Khen Han Ming

1

"Be Prepared... the meaning of the motto is that a scout must prepare himself by previous thinking out and practicing how to act on any accident or emergency so that he is never taken by surprise..."

- *Robert Baden-Powell*

ABOUT THIS BOOK

Terrorist attacks such as those in Mumbai, Paris, Brussels, Tunisia, Philippines and Indonesia with the utilization of powerful weapons and explosives have been intended to inflict losses. Such attacks are usually defined by traditional methods that target a single site and are designed to inflict maximum casualties and fatalities by causing devastation and disruption in our day to day livelihood and financial impact whilst gaining media attention.

This book is aimed at providing readers with the vital information and advice to help keep themselves safe, as well as practical guidance on the information required by emergency responders. How should you respond if your business or organization is the target for an attack, or is affected by a nearby incident?

The objective of this book is to provide as much information and awareness to first responders on such incidents and the damaging consequences by offering information on such incidents and provides advice designed to assist in a rapid return to normality to minimize business losses.

3

Dedication

This book is dedicated to all the brave men and women who gave their lives in the line of duty... and those who stood up against violence and extremism.

Author, Khen Han Ming at the site of the 2016 Jakarta attacks near the Sarinah shopping mall in central Jakarta.

Table of Contents

WHAT IF...

You wake up one day and you suddenly realize that:

You are caught in the midst of a terrorist attack, OR

You are among the first to observe or discover a suspected terrorist activity and have to notify the authorities?

Under such circumstances, it is a whole lot better if you have:

- Basic awareness of what terrorism is and the risks involved;
- Knowledge of the anticipated consequences of a terrorist incident;
- Recognizing terrorism (or is it just a regular criminal activity?);
- Familiarity with the requirement for additional resources, and how to escalate to an emergency communication center; and;
- The competency to self-protect, keeping your safety as a priority.

SAFETY FIRST!

By all means, your safety should be the utmost concern and priority in order to protect yourself.

In the event that you become injured in any way, you may not be able to call for an immediate help or assistance which means that you need to attend to the situation in order to weigh in on the immediate issues of the incident scene.

Whenever available, such as the use of personal protective equipment (PPE) paired with positive pressure self-contained breathing apparatus (SCBA) will tremendously contribute to your safety level.

If you are a member of an emergency operations team, you must be well organized and equipped in order to be successful.

Teamwork is key!

One of the best ways to understand the nature of organization is to picture it from a methodical approach: from a unit of correlated, dependent components or activity which are devised in order to achieve a common purpose.

In the event should you presume a chemical, biological, or nuclear incident, this book is in no way meant to prepare you with the adequate training in order to completely protect yourself.

Your main role and responsibility in this situation is to immediately contact the authorities.

Terrorism in Perspective

The threat is REAL

Terrorists have the knowledge and the capability to strike anywhere in the world.

Yes, that is an astounding fact.

According to history, when properly motivated, they will do whatever in order to accomplish their objectives.

From a modern perspective, the tragic events of September 11 in 2001, and the anthrax attacks thereafter were wake-up calls for all of us, citizens of the world!

There were also other notable bombing incidents such as the 1996 Olympics, the 2003 and 2009 Jakarta Marriott bombings, the 2005 London bombings and the 2013 Boston Marathon bombing.

And there's the war in Iraq and Syria, as well as the battle of Marawi in the Philippines. Lest we forget, the numerous separatist movement and skirmish attacks in parts of India, Pakistan, Northern Ireland and the southern provinces of Thailand.

There have been many, numerous smaller occurrences, some of which techniques used were unconventional and low-tech or crude and does not include the utilization of high powered weapons or sophisticated explosives:

- A terrorist ploughed through a van into groups of people, murdering 13 individuals and injuring more than a hundred people in Barcelona's Las Ramblas on August 17, 2017.
- A van driver mowed down Muslim worshippers on Seven Sisters Road near Finsbury Park mosque in the early morning of June 19, 2017.
- The London Bridge terror attack killed eight people and injured many others on London Bridge and in nearby Borough Market on June 3, 2017.
- Manchester terror attack on May 22, 2017 killed at least 22 people and injured 59 others at the Ariana Grande concert at Manchester Arena.
- Paris shooting on April 20, 2017 killing a policeman injuring two others at the Champs Elysees Avenue.
- A man drove a truck down a busy shopping street in central Stockholm

killing four people and wounded at least fifteen others on April 7, 2017.

- The Brussels bombings slaughtered 32 individuals and injured in excess of 300 other victims on March 22, 2016. Two suicide bombings at the Brussels Airport and another bombing at a Metro station in the Belgium capital.
- Charlie Hebdo attack on January 7, 2015 where two masked gunmen attacked the French satirical weekly newspaper in Paris. 12 people were killed on that day. A policeman was killed the day after and four hostages were killed on January 9 at a Jewish supermarket.

These episodes represent the strategies just as the objectives of terrorism, which can nearly be anybody.

The list will continue to grow.

A popular view on why there have not been further large-scale attacks in the US (such as the September 11 attacks) is that terrorists are attempting to kill Americans overseas, such as in Europe, Asia and particularly in Afghanistan and Iraq.

Greater cooperation and coordination at all levels has implied that numerous terrorism incidents have been effectively prevented.

All communities, especially those in free societies – are defenseless and vulnerable to terrorism, as nearly all of these communities contain some exceptionally obvious target.

For example, many may have manufacturing and testing facilities.

Other instances of places that may be targets for terrorist activity include:

- Public assembly;
- Public structures;
- Mass Transit Systems;
- Places with high rise economic impact;
- Telecommunications offices; and
- Places with historical, emblematic or symbolic significance

Despite our security consciousness and levels of readiness, if terrorists plan to wreak havoc and unleash devastation, it will be hard to stop them.

An act of terrorism can take place at any moment, particularly when you would least expect it to happen.

What is terrorism?

A good reference to the definition of terrorism can be found in the now-repealed Malaysian Internal Security Act (or ISA) 1960 [ACT 82]:

"terrorist" means any person who--

(a)   by the use of any fire-arm, explosive or ammunition acts in a manner prejudicial to the public safety or to the maintenance of public order or incites to violence or counsels disobedience to the law or to any lawful order;

(b)   carries or has in his possession or under his control any fire-arm, ammunition or explosive without lawful authority thereof; or

(c) demands, collects or receives any supplies for the use of any person who intends or is about to act, or has recently acted, in a manner prejudicial to public safety or the maintenance of public order.

According to the Security Offences (Special Measures) Act (or SOSMA) 2012 [Act 747], the act of "terrorism" is defined as:

1) To cause, or to cause a substantial number of citizens to fear, organized violence against persons or property;

2) An act which is prejudicial to public order in, or the security of, the Federation or any part thereof;

3) Procure the alteration, otherwise than by lawful means, of anything by law established

Definition under the Malaysian National Security Council (NSC) states that:

"Terrorism is the unlawful use of threat or the use of force or terror or any other attack by a person, group or state regardless of objective or justification aimed at another state, its citizens or their properties and its vital services with the intention of creating fear, intimidation and thus forcing governments or organizations to follow their impressed will including those acts in support directly or indirectly" (please refer to Directive No. 18, issued by the NSC).

According to the US definition, as contained in Part 18 of the United States Code for Crimes and Criminal Procedure, it differentiates between "international terrorism" and "domestic terrorism".

Under "international terrorism", it is defined as: "Violent acts or acts dangerous to human life that violate federal or state law and appear to be intended to intimidate or coerce a civilian population; to influence the policy of a government by intimidation or coercion; or to affect the conduct of a government by mass destruction, assassination, or kidnapping; and occur primarily outside the territorial jurisdiction of the US, or transcend national boundaries."

Domestic terrorism, on the other hand, is defined as: "Acts dangerous to human life that violate federal or state law and appear to intended to intimidate or coerce a civilian population; to influence the policy of a government by intimidation or coercion; or to affect the conduct of a government by mass destruction, assassination or kidnapping; and occur primarily within the territorial jurisdiction of the US."

The United States Federal Bureau of Investigation (FBI) also defines terrorism as: "Terrorism is 'the unlawful use of force against persons or property to intimidate or coerce a government, the civilian population, or any segment of thereof, in the furtherance of political or social objectives.'

This includes three elements:

- ✓ Terrorist activities are illegal and involve the use of force.
- ✓ The actions intend to intimidate or coerce.
- ✓ The actions are committed in support of political or social objectives.

Global understanding of the term

'terrorism'

The United Nations defines "terrorism" in Resolution 1566 (2004):

... criminal acts, including acts against civilians, committed with intent to cause death or serious bodily injury, or taking of hostages, with the purpose to provoke a state of terror in the general public or in a group of persons or particular persons, intimidate a population or compel a government or an international organization to do or to abstain from doing any act, which constitute offences within the scope of and as defined in the international conventions and protocols relating to terrorism, are under no circumstances justifiable by considerations of a political, philosophical, ideological, racial, ethnic, religious or other similar nature, and calls upon all States to prevent such acts and, if not prevented, to ensure that such acts are punished by penalties consistent with their grave nature."

In many countries, terrorism is considered the greatest, or one of the biggest dangers impacting relationships between nations and between communities.

Some may contend that we live in a post nine eleven world, because of its colossal impact on connections which influences the manner in which we consider security. You may feel free to concur or differ with this statement.

Terrorism is a worldwide phenomenon but there are huge regional contrasts which gives impact on the overall peace and security.

Due to these distinctions, we presently can't seem to come to a common agreement with respect to the meaning of 'terrorism' as a term, which implies that different governments may consider interpreting certain acts of terrorism differently, which also incorporates the classifying of various terrorist groups.

One should be mindful that the acts of terrorism are indeed acts of crime, BUT not all crimes are considered terrorism.

What is a threat?

The most commonly used meaning of a terrorist or criminal threat generally has five components:

1. **Willful Threat**
   When someone threatens to initiate steps to carry out an action made in writing, verbally or electronically transmitted that the intended target will result in death or great bodily harm, the threat clearly has to be of an exceptionally dangerous nature.

2. **Specific Intent**
   The threat was made with the particular plan that it be taken as a threat. Although this surely appears like a redundant sentence, it is intended to pass on the message that the threat is a crime even if there is no actual intent to carry it out. The main goal you need is simply the aim to make the threat itself. So in the event that a perpetrator plans to blow up a facility, he or she will be in any case liable of this crime regardless if one is totally unarmed and have no means of achieving this by any means.

3. Unequivocal, Unconditional, and Specific

The threat is unequivocal, unconditional, and specific as to pass on a gravity of purpose and prompt prospect of execution. This inconceivably muddled sounding sentence is basic to the law, so let's break it down:

- Unequivocal implies that the danger must be an immediate articulation of what you will do, instead of can do.
- Unconditional is rarely used in light that it is a gray area as it doesn't indicate a fixed circumstance in which a threat will be executed yet probably, the less the conditions used, the more probable the court will rule that it is a threat.
- Specific alludes to dangers that are evident and can't be dubious.

4. Caused Fear

The threat actually caused fear in the victim and people must actually believe your threat for you to be arrested for it.

5. **The Fear Was Reasonable**
   If you said that you are going to blow up an important landmark with your spaceship, it is very unlikely that any reasonable person could take this seriously.

A threat generally consists of two elements: motive and ability.

Principally, determining the threat is a law enforcement function. On a more practical level, however emergency responders must realize that it is also possible for anyone to perpetrate an act of terrorism.

Criminal component is the most important factor that separates a terrorist organization and its actions from that of a legitimate organization.

We should also be mindful on the existence of several domestic terrorist organizations which are often considered to be violent extremist groups that fringes on legitimate, constitutionally-protected organizations.

At the time of writing and editing this book, French butchers have called on the government to protect them against violent attacks from vegan "terrorism" as some butcher shops across France have had rocks and fake blood thrown on their storefronts.

A vegan militant was also found guilty of apologizing for terrorism after a butcher from Super U supermarket was killed in a March 2018 terror attack in Trèbes, south-west of France.

Terrorists can also act alone.

A reasonably preferred standpoint for a terrorist to act alone is that the individual can't be easily infiltrated or intercepted by our law enforcement agencies due to the absence of data or intelligence.

Such events could be extremely lethal as it is intended to inflict harm and damage.

Fire resulting from a careless smoker's indiscriminate act of littering was probably not set with the intention to damage, hurt, or killing somebody.

There are exceptions, however, in the case of arson.

Terrorists will try to make sure that the event has its full impact, even when it means destroying a whole building and killing all of its occupants.

Recent bombing incidents showed that there can be a sequence of events carefully timed to inflict further harm on the authorities, which proves that terrorists will do almost anything in order to achieve their ends.

Some additional hazards will include:

✓ Armed resistance;
✓ Use of weapons;
✓ Booby Traps; and
✓ Secondary events

Experts have said that there are five categories of terrorist incidents in general: Biological, Nuclear, Incendiary, Chemical and Explosive.

This is where the acronym **B-NICE** comes from. It is a simple way to remember the five categories.

But, don't limit your planning by these acronyms: neither one includes armed attack in their categories of incidents, yet this is a very effective tool in dealing with terrorist attacks.

Realize also that terrorists must constantly adapt their techniques in order to succeed in their mission.

We must not discount the potential for newer techniques or modes of attack that were never used before in the past. This will require some out of the box thinking in order to assess the situation.

It is important to understand the 4 routes of entry: inhalation, absorption, ingestion and injection.

Whenever possible, you should exercise good judgment in using personal protective equipment (PPE) provided/available.

The use of protective clothing, including positive-pressure, self-contained breathing apparatus (PP-SCBA), will definitely enhance your safety.

An Overview

Biological incidents.

Some biological agents have the potential to be used as tools for terrorism such as anthrax (which are sometimes found in sheep, cows and other hoofed animals), tularemia (or rabbit fever), cholera, encephalitis, the plague (which typically spread from rodents to humans from flea bites), and botulism (usually found in improperly canned food which can be naturally occurring or they can be specifically grown or manufactured in a laboratory).

We should be cautious on the dangers of biological agents that:

- ✓ Pose genuine threats given their fairly open nature, and the quick widespread potential for infecting mass casualties.
- ✓ They are disseminated by the use of aerosols (spray devices), oral (contaminating food or water supplies), dermal (direct skin contact with the substance, or injection).
- ✓ Are intrinsically more dangerous than most chemical agents, and they

29

are possibly more effective for terrorists to use because most biological agents are naturally occurring organisms – such as bacteria and viruses (microbes and infections).

✓ Are self-reproducing and have explicit physiologically-focused effects. Additionally, terrorists can utilize them against plants, animals, people or materials (for example, foodstuffs). Through food contamination (or to a lesser extent contamination of water supplies), terrorists can cause massive disruptions and illness.

According to the US Centers for Disease Control and Prevention (CDC), **Category A Agents** are considered the most dangerous biological agents because:

1. They can be easily disseminated or transmitted from person to person.
2. They result in high mortality rates and have the potential for major public health impact.
3. They might cause public panic and social disruption requiring special action such as a specific vaccine or public health preparedness.

These agents are:

- ✓ Anthrax (Bacillus anthracis);
- ✓ Botulism (Clostridium botulinum toxin);
- ✓ Plague (Yersinia pestis);
- ✓ Smallpox (variola major);
- ✓ Tularemia (Francisella tularensis); and
- ✓ Viral hemorrhagic fevers (filoviruses (e.g., Ebola, Marburg) and arenaviruses (e.g., Lassa, Machupo)).

In general, there are four common types of biological agents:

- ✓ Bacteria
- ✓ Viruses
- ✓ Rickettsia and;
- ✓ Toxins

Bacteria and Rickettsia

Bacteria are single-celled organisms that multiply by cell division and causes disease in humans, plants or animals, while rickettsia are smaller than bacteria and live inside individual host cells.

Examples of bacteria include anthrax (Bacillus Anthracis), cholera (Vibrio Cholerae), plague (Yersinia Pestis), tularemia (Francisella Tularensis).

Examples of rickettsial infections and related infections are anaplasmosis, ehrlichiosis and Q fever (Coxiella Burnetii) which are caused by an unusual type of bacteria that can live only inside the cells of another organism.

The anthrax disease is commonly associated with cows, sheep and horses serving as hosts.

Handling of contaminated hair, wool, hides, flesh, or other animal substances can lead to contracting cutaneous (dermal) anthrax.

Intentional dissemination of spores via aerosol, such as for terroristic purposes, is another way people could contract it and cause a more dangerous form of the disease such as inhalational anthrax.

The anthrax incidents of 2001 which have become known as "one of the largest and most complex in the history of law enforcement" came following days after the September 11 attacks illustrated just how effective this agent could be.

The US Federal Bureau of Investigation (FBI) have given the 2001 anthrax attacks a case name, known as Amerithrax when letters containing anthrax spores were mailed to several news agencies and at least two US senators which resulted in killing 5 people and infecting over 17 others.

The attacks also generated thousands of 'suspicious white powder' calls that turned out to be harmless substances.

Virus

Viruses are the simplest type of microorganisms that lacks a system for their own metabolism and depend upon living cells to multiply.

In other words, viruses will not live long outside of their hosts.

Types of viruses that could fill in as biological agents include smallpox, Venezuelan equine encephalitis, the viral hemorrhagic fevers such as the Ebola, Marburg infections and the Lassa fever.

According to the US CDC, "smallpox is a serious, contagious, and sometimes fatal infectious disease. There is no specific treatment for smallpox disease, and the only prevention is vaccination."

The fatality rate is estimated to be between 10 and 30%.

Historically, it was the reason for many fatalities and because of an extensive international public health effort smallpox was eradicated in 1978.

The last recorded case of smallpox in the United States was in 1949 when Lilian Barber, then 43, was the only person to die in the last smallpox outbreak in the US, which infected eight victims in the Rio Grande Valley.

Governments around the world continue to be vigilant in monitoring and preparation for a few reasons:

1. Since the US doesn't have any ongoing, recent background with smallpox, there may be difficulties with medical practitioners making a correct diagnosis.
2. In April 1972, the international community agreed on a comprehensive ban on the development, production and stockpiling biological weapons.
3. Although the major stockpiles of smallpox that were developed for biological weapons have been destroyed, there are still two countries with legal smallpox research supplies: the United States and the Russian Federation. However, it is also believed that several countries, too, are maintaining illegal smallpox inventories, such as Iran and North Korea.

Immunization is yet thought to be the only effective protection, besides antiviral medications which have additionally appeared to have some incentive as indicated by research.

Since the introduction of vaccination (for smallpox) by Edward Jenner over 200 years ago, the World Health Organization (WHO) announced that nine major diseases affecting mankind have been controlled to a greater or lesser extent through the use of vaccines.

Interestingly, it is believed that the Soviet Union may have successfully developed a "chimera," or a hybrid virus. The first plan back then was with smallpox and another virus, by inserting the equine encephalomyelitis (VEE) genes into smallpox. Using the same techniques, a chimera strain of ectromelia and VEE was created for initial testing during the late 1980's.

The tests resulted in this chimera strain producing symptoms of both ectromelia and VEE in lab animals.

Following the collapse of the Soviet Union in early 1992, Russian President Boris

Yel'tsin decreed to cease all biological weapons-related activity.

There was a considerable amount of downsizing in this area, which included the destruction of existing biological weapons reserve. There still remains question, however, that Russia has totally dismantled the old Soviet program.

Toxins

Toxins are defined as any harmful or poisonous substance produced by a living organism (such as bees, snakes, and sea urchins), which can be dangerous to human.

They are different from other chemical agents in that they are not manmade and they have a much more complex component.

Synthetic toxic substances added or introduced into the environment by people, on the other hand, are called toxicants.

Toxins can be easily extracted for use as a terrorist weapon, and by weight, usually are more toxic than many chemical agents.

The 4 common toxins which has the potential to be used as biological agents:

botulism (botulinum), SEB (staphylococcal enterotoxin B), ricin, and mycotoxins.

According to the US CDC, botulism is "a rare but serious paralytic illness caused by a nerve toxin that is produced by the bacterium *Clostridium botulinum*."

Although there are 3 main kinds of botulism, foodborne botulism is probably the most adaptable to terrorist use and is caused by eating foods that contain the botulism toxin.

Ricin is a toxin derived from the castor bean plant, available worldwide. There have been several documented cases involving ricin throughout the United States, particularly in rural areas.

Routes of Exposure

Primary routes of exposure for biological agents are inhalation and ingestion. Skin absorption and injection also are potential routes of entry, but are less likely.

In order to determine the risk of harmful health effects from a toxin, you must first know how toxic substance is, how much, and by what means, a person becomes exposed and how sensitive is that person to the substance.

The route of exposure can determine whether or not the toxic substance has an effect.

Not everyone is equally sensitive to toxins and chemicals, and is not affected by it the same way. There are several reasons for this:

1. Genetic factors can cause one's body's ability to react, break down or eliminate certain chemicals.
2. Age, illness, diet, alcohol use, pregnancy, medical or non-medical drug use can also affect a person's sensitivity to toxins and chemicals.

Treatment

Treatment should only be administered by qualified medical professionals and is specific for each biological agent.

Generally, treatments include pharmaceuticals, such as antibiotics and antivirals; as well as vaccinations.

Nuclear Incidents

There are basically two different threats from of nuclear terrorism:

1. The use, threatened use, or threatened detonation, of a nuclear bomb, and;
2. The detonation, or threatened detonation, of conventional explosive incorporating nuclear materials (radiological dispersal devices or RDD).

It is unlikely that any terrorist organization could acquire or build a nuclear device, or acquire and use a fully functional nuclear weapon.

The number of nations with nuclear capability is relatively small, and each places a very high priority on the control of its nuclear weapons.

Even if a nation supporting terrorism could develop a nuclear capability, it would be implausible for that nation to turn a completed weapon over to a group that might possibly use it against them.

The question of probability of theft of a completed nuclear weapon is also highly

unlikely because all western and former
Soviet nuclear weapons are protected with a
Permissible Action Link (PAL) system that
renders the weapon harmless until a proper
code is entered.

RECAP!

Theft or manufacture of a nuclear weapon is very unlikely, but it is still a major concern due to the detonation of such a device's impact: environmentally, socially, and medically.

Such a detonation would cause massive numbers of deaths and casualties such as burn cases, trauma injuries, and acute radiation sicknesses.

Electromagnetic fields, on the other hand, would be disrupted to the extent that all computer and communication systems would go completely offline!

The greatest potential terrorist threat for a nuclear weapon would be to use it as a form of extortion against the government.

Presently, there is no known instance of any private organizations or groups close to obtaining or producing a nuclear weapon. However, with the fall of the Soviet Union in 1991, many of the country's nuclear devices are 'unaccounted for.'

Nuclear materials incorporated into Radiological Dispersal Devices (RDD) would be used to spread radioactive materials around the bomb site.

This would disrupt normal, day-to-day activities, and would raise the level of concern among first responders regarding long-term health issues and it would be difficult to perform complete environmental decontamination.

Nuclear materials detonated by a large device, such as a truck bomb (large vehicle with high quantities of explosives) in the vicinity of a nuclear power plant or a radiological cargo in transport can have similar impacts.

Another scenario is the use an aircraft to crash into a nuclear power plant's spent fuel rods. Such an attack could have widespread effects.

We should be mindful that there is an increasing frequency of radioactive materials shipment throughout the world.

There are 3 main types of nuclear radiation emitted from radioactive materials: alpha, beta, and gamma radiation.

Alpha particles are the heaviest and most highly charged of the nuclear particles.

However, alpha particles cannot travel more than a few inches in the air and are completely stopped by an ordinary sheet of paper. The outermost layer of dead skin that covers the body can stop even the most energetic alpha particle. But if ingested through eating, drinking, or breathing contaminated materials, they can become an internal hazard.

Beta particles are smaller and travel much faster than alpha particles. Typical beta particles can travel several millimeters through tissue, but they generally do not penetrate far enough to reach the vital inner organs.

Exposure to beta particles from outside the body is normally thought of as a slight hazard. But if the skin is exposed to large amounts of beta radiation for long periods of time, skin burns may result. If removed from the skin shortly after exposure, beta-emitting materials will not cause serious burns. Like alpha particles, beta particles are considered to be an internal hazard if taken into the body by eating, drinking, or breathing contaminated materials. Beta-emitting contamination also can enter the body through unprotected open wounds.

Gamma rays are a type of electromagnetic radiation transmitted through space in the form of waves, which are pure energy and therefore the most penetrating type of radiation.

They can travel great distances and can penetrate most materials. This creates a problem for humans because gamma rays can attack all tissues and organs. Gamma radiation has very distinctive, short-term symptoms.

Acute radiation sickness occurs when an individual is exposed to a large amount of radiation within a short period of time. Symptoms of acute radiation sickness include skin irritation, nausea, vomiting, high fever, hair loss and dermal burns.

Incendiary incidents

Usually, crime scene investigators find 3 types of incendiary devices: electrical, mechanical, or chemical which are typically deployed in targeted attacks with the intention to cause fires.

A single delay mechanism may also be used or in combination with other combustible materials that burn with a hot flame for a designated period of time.

The main aim of such attacks is to set materials or structures in fire.

Incendiary devices come in all shapes and sizes, simple or elaborate. The type of device is limited only by the terrorist's imagination and ingenuity.

An incendiary device can be a simple match applied to a piece of paper, or a matchbook-and-cigarette arrangement, or a complicated self-igniting chemical device.

The airplanes used in the September 11 attacks, for example, were essentially huge incendiary devices loaded with aviation fuel.

Normally an incendiary device is a material or mixture of materials designed to produce enough heat and flame in order to cause combustible material to burn once it reaches its ignition temperature.

Each device consists of 3 basic components: an igniter or fuse, a container or body, and an incendiary material or filler.

The container can be glass, metal, plastic or paper depending on its desired use.

A device containing chemical materials will usually be in a metal or other non-breakable container.

An incendiary device that uses a liquid accelerator usually will be in a breakable container, e.g., glass.

Only specially trained personnel should handle incendiary devices discovered prior to ignition, as handling of such devices by inexperienced individuals can result in ignition and possibly lead to severe injuries or death.

Chemical incidents

There are generally 5 classes of chemical agents:

1. **Nerve agents**, which are used to disrupt nerve impulse transmissions;
2. **Blister agents**, also called vesicants, causes severe burns to the eyes, skin, and tissues of the respiratory tract;
3. **Blood agents**, which interferes the ability of blood to transport oxygen;
4. **Choking agents**, which causes respiratory distress and tearing, designed to incapacitate.
5. **Irritating agents** or also known as **Riot Control Agents**, which causes intense pain to the skin, especially in moist areas of the body.

Nerve Agents

Nerve agents are chemicals that affect the nervous system, similar in nature to organophosphate pesticides, but with a higher degree of toxicity. These agents are man-made and have been manufactured for chemical warfare.

Many of these were initially developed as insecticides and have been known to be kept in military stockpiles of several countries, including the United States.

Generally, nerve agents resemble water or light oil in pure form and possess no odor, liquid in room temperature and are highly toxic even in small concentrations, which can be mixed easily with water and other solvents.

The agents, which include sarin (GB) were used by terrorists against Japanese civilians and by the Iraqis against Iran; Soman (GD), Tabun (GA); and V agent (VX).

These materials are typically sprayed as an aerosol for dissemination. Small explosions and equipment to generate mists (spray devices) may be present.

A chemical attack in the Syrian city of Douma on April 7, 2018 reportedly killed at least 70 people. On-site medics said a mixture of chlorine gas and sarin was used in the attack.

In case of GA, GB and GD, the first letter 'G' refers to the country (Germany) that developed the agent, and the second letter indicate the order of development. "GC" was skipped as an acronym because in that era it was the medical abbreviation for gonorrhea.

In this case of VX, this was named by the British, the "V" stands for "venom" while the "X" represents one of the chemicals in the specific compound.

The assassination of Kim Jong Nam, the eldest son of North Korean Leader Kim Jong-il on February 13, 2017 at the Kuala Lumpur International Airport was believed to be conducted by North Korean agents using the VX nerve agent.

The victims' symptoms will be an early warning sign of the use of nerve agents. There are various generic symptoms similar to organophosphate poisoning. The victims will salivate, lacrimate, urinate and defecate without much control.

Indicators and symptoms of nerve agent poisoning include:

- ✓ Eyes: pinpointed pupils, dimmed and blurred vision, pain aggravated by sunlight;
- ✓ Skin: excessive sweating and fine muscle tremors'
- ✓ Muscles: involuntary twitching and contractions;
- ✓ Respiratory system: runny nose and nasal congestion, chest pressure and congestion, coughing and difficulty in breathing;
- ✓ Digestive system: excessive salivation, abdominal pain, nausea and vomiting, involuntary defecation and urination'; and
- ✓ Nervous system: giddiness, anxiety, difficulty in thinking and sleeping (nightmares).

Nerve agents kill insect life, birds and other animals as well as humans. Many dead animals at the scene of an incident may be another outward warning sign or indicator.

Treatment generally includes immediate decontamination, administration of atropine and pralidoxime.

Blister Agents

Blister agents are also known as mustard agents due to their characteristic smell, which resembles the common yellow 'hot dog' mustard odor.

They appear to be very similar to other corrosive materials, with the ability to penetrate layers of clothing and are quickly absorbed into skin.

Blister agents are heavy, oily liquids, typically dispersed by aerosol or vaporization, so small explosions or spray equipment may be present.

In a pure state, they are nearly colorless and odorless, but slight impurities give them a dark color and pungent odor similar to mustard, garlic, or onions. Although volatility is low, vapors can reach hazardous levels during warm weather.

Mustard (H, HD), and lewisite (L) are common blister agents which are very toxic, although in a much lesser degree compared to nerve agents.

A few drops on the skin can cause severe injury, while at least 3 grams absorbed through the skin can be fatal.

Clinical symptoms may not appear for hours or days.

Indicators and symptoms of blister agents include:

- ✓ Eyes: reddening, congestion, tearing, burning, and a 'gritty' feeling; in severe cases, swelling of the eyelids, severe pain, and spasm of the eyelids;
- ✓ Skin: within 1 to 12 hours, initial mild itching followed by redness, tenderness, and burning pain, followed by burns and fluid-filled blisters. The effects are enhanced in the warm, moist areas of the groin and armpits;
- ✓ Respiratory system: within 2 to 12 hours, burning sensation in the nose and throat, hoarseness, profusely running nose, severe cough, and shortness of breath; and
- ✓ Digestive system: within 2 to 3 hours, abdominal pain, nausea, blood-stained vomiting, and bloody diarrhea.

Outward signs of blister agents include complaints of eye and respiratory irritation along with reports of a garlic-like odor.

53

Similar symptoms will occur among many individuals exposed. As the blister break, infection prevention becomes a high priority.

Treatment in general includes immediate decontamination.

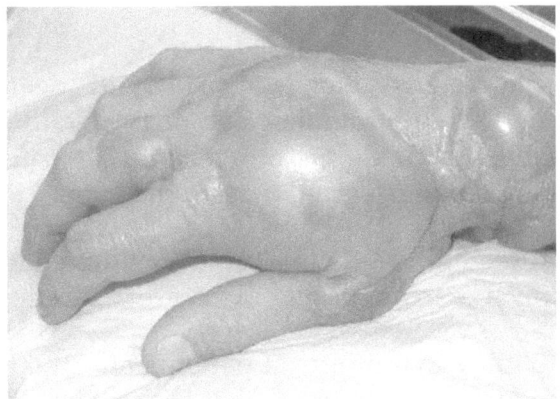

Skin blisters from mustard gas attack

Blood Agents

Blood agents interfere with the ability of the blood to transport oxygen, resulting in asphyxiation.

Common blood agents include: hydrogen cyanide (AC) and cyanogens chloride (CK).

All blood agents are toxic at high concentrations and lead to rapid death. Some, such as cyanides, can cause fatalities in seconds. CK, on the other hand, can cause tearing of the eyes and irritate the lungs.

Affected persons require immediate removal to fresh air and respiratory therapy.

Clinical symptoms of patients affected by blood agents include:

- ✓ Respiratory distress;
- ✓ Vomiting and diarrhea; and
- ✓ Vertigo and headaches.

Under pressure, blood agents are liquids. In pure form, they are gasses. Precursor chemicals are typically cyanide salts and acids. All have the aroma of bitter almonds or peach blossoms. They are common industrial chemicals and are readily available.

Treatment should be rendered by medical professionals, generally includes immediate decontamination and for cyanides; the administration of amyl nitrite.

Choking Agents

Pulmonary agents, also known as choking agents are chemical weapons that stress the respiratory tract, disrupting a victim's natural ability to breathe.

Severe distress causes pulmonary edema, or fluid in the lungs, which can result in asphyxiation similar to drowning.

Chlorine and phosgene, common industrial chemicals, are choking agents. Clinical symptoms include severe eye irritation and respiratory distress (coughing and choking). Most people recognize the odor of chlorine, while Phosgene has the odor of newly cut hay.

As both are gases, they are stored and transported in bottles or cylinders. Treatment generally includes immediate decontamination and ventilation assistance with oxygen.

Irritating Agents

Irritating agents, such as riot control agents or tear gas, are designed to incapacitate. Generally, they are nonlethal; however, they can result in asphyxiation under certain circumstances and could be used to create disruption or panic.

Common irritating agents: chloropicrin, MACE (CN), tear gas (CS), capsicum/pepper spray, and dibenzoxazepine (CR).

Clinical symptoms typically include:

- ✓ Eyes and throat: burning or irritation;
- ✓ Respiratory system: respiratory distress, coughing, choking, and difficulty breathing; and
- ✓ Digestive system: high concentrations may lead to nausea and vomiting.

These agents can cause pain, sometimes severe, on skin, especially in moist areas.

Most exposed persons report the odor of pepper or of tear gas. Outward warning signs include the odour of these agents and the presence of dispensing devices. Many are available over the counter.

Treatment generally includes immediate decontamination.

The primary routes of exposure for chemical agents are inhalation, ingestion, and skin absorption/contact. Injection is a potential source of entry but is less likely.

With the exception of blister agents, inhalation is the primary route of exposure for chemical agents. Skin absorption/contact with irritant nerve agents and blister agents also a highly possible route of exposure.

Explosive Incidents

Explosives are generally defined into one of these 2 categories:

1) Any substance or article, including a device, designated to function by explosion (e.g., an extremely rapid release of gas and heat); or
2) Any substance or article, including a device, which, by chemical reaction within itself, can function in a similar manner even if not designed to function by explosion, unless the substance or article is otherwise classified.

Why is there a particular concern about the use of explosives?

The design of any improvised explosive devices (IED) are limited only to the imagination of the bomb maker, thus can take any form, size or appearance.

Particularly because their extensive use in vehicle-borne explosives (VBIED) incidents, it is a major issue as the results are large numbers of fatalities and injuries, including structural collapses.

Responders were also targeted by secondary devices.

There are 3 other interesting facts about explosives:

1) When law enforcement and public safety agencies know of the presence of such a device, they usually have only a 20 % chance of finding it.
2) Hundreds more 'hoax' bomb incidents are reported each year.
3) Residential properties are the most common targets for bombers.

The conclusion is that improvised explosives and incendiary devices are designed and assembled to explode and cause fire.

Explosions rapidly release gas and heat, affecting both structures and people.

Bombings are the types of terrorist attacks most likely to be encountered. Bombs nearly always work as designed. An important point to remember is that explosions can cause fires, and fires can cause explosions.

The 5 types of incidents previously discussed are similar, in some respects, to routine emergencies.

You still can protect yourselves using sound judgment and the basic equipments.

Aftermath of the 2008 Islamabad Marriott bombing carried out by a VBIED which killed at least 54 people, injuring at least 266 others and left a 20m x 6m crater outside the hotel.

UNDERSTAND THIS

Today, emergency responders and others in emergency services are increasingly facing new challenges that seriously affect not only the public but those very persons whose job it is to help and protect the public.

The risks pose threats for which the average emergency responder may not be fully prepared for.

Responders should obtain assistance in identifying the chemicals from container shapes, placards, labels, shipping papers, and analytical tests.

These threats go far beyond the usual ones associated with residential fires, vehicular accidents, or even hazardous materials incidents.

It is critical that you understand the implications of these modern threats and know proper response procedures and the limits of safe and prudent response.

Your knowledge will help prevent further fatalities.

The emergency services community has tremendous knowledge and resources available from the government, military, public health, and law enforcement agencies, to name some of the more obvious.

RECOGNIZING THE SIGNS

Assuring a safe response to a potential crime scene

There are many similarities between terrorism scene responses and the more common crime scenes to which public safety agencies respond.

While law enforcement officers are well versed in crime scene investigations, the majority of fire, emergency medical services (EMS), military, and emergency management personnel may not be at par.

To begin with, always maintain situational awareness – not just on calls that may be suspicious – but on any calls!

Your situational awareness may be based on information from communicators, personnel already on scene, from your initial or later observations, or other sources.

Any responses to an incident other than a natural disaster may be a response to a crime scene.

Most often, your response will be to an incident that will be categorized as something other than terrorism.

There are many reasons for this. Here are two examples:

1) Terrorists rarely 'pre-warn' or announce that they are planning to carry out a terrorism incident at a particular time and location, or of a particular type in advance.
2) Although the specific methodology and definition of a terrorism incident may be quite broad, it could be masked as a non-terrorism incident: a chemical spill as an industrial accident or a disease outbreak as a natural occurrence. For example,

firefighters may be first responders to arson scenes, EMS personnel or community volunteers may be called upon to administer aid to victims of a violent crime. Hazardous materials teams also frequently respond to sites of clandestine dumping or intentional releases of chemicals.

At the site of incident, you will need to coordinate closely with other first-responding fire, EMS, and law enforcement personnel in order to ensure that you do not destroy important evidence and that you stay safe.

You may also have to coordinate with public health and military personnel, public works, elected officials, public information officers, volunteer groups (including NGOs), the media and others.

Remember that even when the emergency phase of the incident is over, the incident itself has not ended.

The incident ends only when there is successful prosecution of the guilty person(s).

It may, in fact, be years before all perpetrators are captured, prosecuted, and appeals are completed. You should be aware of warning signs that indicate a potential criminal activity, because some incidents will involve criminal acts.

Avoid Impeding the Investigation

Be sure to coordinate your actions with law enforcement operations.

Basically, there are 3 ways to help solve a crime:

1) The confession of the perpetrator,
2) Statements provided by witnesses or victims, and;
3) Incriminating information obtained through physical evidence which provides incontestable, impartial facts (beyond reasonable doubt).

Only physical evidence can overcome the conflicting and confusing statements of witnesses who, observing the same incident at essentially the same time, nonetheless have different perceptions of what took place.

Physical evidence may be crucial to connect the perpetrator to the scene. The recognition, collection and preservation of physical evidence may be the only means to identify, and successfully prosecute, those responsible.

Your job is not to collect evidence, but to simply recognize and preserve it. NOT touching such an object, while noting its location, serves both those functions.

Keep this in mind when arriving at any potential crime scene.

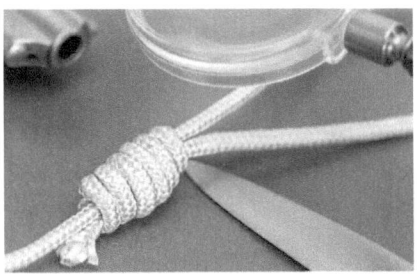

If you are involved with a terrorist incident as a first responder, you essentially become part of the crime scene. As they do with any material witness, law enforcement personnel likely will interview you at some point. You may be required to testify in court as to what you saw, did, and did not do. Thus, writing down your observations as soon as it is safe to do so may be important. Remember that such notes may be entered into evidence. Sometimes doing something inappropriate is more detrimental to solving the crime than doing nothing at all. Cases have been lost due to imprudent actions of first responders, whether fire, police, or emergency medical responders.

Scene Considerations

Your response to the scene of a potential terrorist attack could involve entry into a hazardous area.

Deadly radioactive, chemical or biological agents already may have contaminated the atmosphere around the scene.

The presence of fires or collapsed building sections may intensify thermal and mechanical risk.

You can hope to survive only by entering this area very carefully: by moving cautiously and by wearing the appropriate personal protective equipment (PPE).

Life safety – including **your life** – is the utmost priority at any scene.

Leave it to the experts

When you suspect hazardous substances or conditions, only qualified personnel are to secure the scene.

Hazardous materials teams typically have an abundant number of detection and monitoring equipments in order to handle the hazard.

Similarly, bomb squad members may have specialized detection and monitoring equipment required to define an explosives hazard.

You should wait for the arrival of traditional resources before attempting entry.

The time can be applied to reevaluate your situational awareness observations.

Any response to the site of a determined mass biological, chemical, or radiological attack may need appropriate decontamination of equipment, entry personnel, survivors, and casualties.

The process of emergency decontamination might be the one of the most crucial exercises that the public safety community can execute during a terrorist incident, and it is also burdensome to the abilities of any level of authority. Therefore it only makes sense for all communities to plan ahead for emergency operations, such as mass decontamination.

Your response to major explosions and fires requires that you pay just as much attention to hazardous conditions as you would at a potential chemical or biological incident.

Always be aware of the possible presence of a secondary device or incident intended to injure or kill you and other first responders.

Often, these secondary devices are referred to as "sucker punch" devices, which are hidden or camouflaged in unsuspecting places such as ordinary objects, vehicles or everyday surrounding items which can be detonated by time delay, radio and cellular devices.

Bombs produce large-scale trauma due to shock waves, projectiles, and structure collapse.

When arriving on the scene of a highly damaged structure, be aware of the structural conditions causing unsafe buildings and the specialized precautions you need to take.

Whatever type of threat you respond to, the description of that you provide to investigators reconstructing the early minutes of activity at the incident can be the key to successful prosecution of the case.

At the scene, be alert of persons coming or going on foot or by vehicle. Jot down the license plate numbers, and brief description of those present.

Encourage witnesses and bystanders to remain calm until investigators have interviewed them and, as needed, they are decontaminated. Note any other unusual circumstances.

Your documentation of the incident will prove invaluable in prosecuting the case.

Whenever possible, provide photographs and video footage to show the 'bigger picture' of the scene.

Include as many details as possible. Use rough sketches to pinpoint the location of the victims and their wounds, as well as the locations of any potential evidence.

Take note on what you see and organize them, include your name and contact information, and provide them to investigators as soon as possible after the response.

In fact, document by using whatever memory aids are available.

Again, bear in mind that any such documentation may be entered as evidence in court.

Leave Things As They Are

At a potential crime scene, it is critical that you disturb the scene as little as possible.

If you absolutely must move something, make sure that you remember where it was placed or located originally, its orientation and condition, and anything else notable. Whenever possible, photograph the object before you move it.

Take notes on any holes, breaks, or scratches that you caused, and pass this information on to the crime scene investigators.

Law enforcement officers must be able to differentiate between the results of the crime and what responders might have done to those results.

Be careful about what you leave behind. Your discarded pieces of cloth, rubber gloves, chewing gum wrapper or cigarette butt, for example, has to be ruled out later by an evidence collection team with better things to do with its time.

You may have to write an after-action report summarizing your activities and observations during the incident.

Be sure to document the report thoroughly using your notes. Remember that **your report can be used in court**, both in your favor and against you.

Locating the Potential Terrorist Threat and Risk Target Assessment

To determine potential terrorist groups active in your organization or jurisdiction, someone need to conduct a threat analysis in cooperation with local, regional, state, and federal law enforcement officials.

This person may be the emergency management coordinator or director, or someone else in the community associated with emergency response.

Terrorist groups may include, but are not limited to, the following:

- ✓ Ethnic separatist and émigré groups;
- ✓ Left-wing radical organizations;
- ✓ Right-wing racist, antiauthority, 'militias', survivalist groups;
- ✓ Small leaderless groups;
- ✓ Foreign terrorist organizations (FTO); and
- ✓ Issue-oriented groups (including animal rights groups, extremist environmental groups, extremist religious groups, anti-tax, anti-authority, anti-abortionists, etc.).

Once such groups are known (threat assessment) the next step is to identify potential facilities or activities that may become targets of terrorist acts.

The following standard assessment criteria list should include:

- ✓ The level of site visibility;
- ✓ The criticality of the site;
- ✓ Accessibility to the site;
- ✓ Hazards materials stored on site; and
- ✓ Number of people (population) at the site.

These facilities may include:

- ✓ Civilian or military government installations;
- ✓ Industries that are part of the 'military-industrial complex', manufacture environmentally sensitive products, operate in politically sensitive countries, or
- ✓ representing capitalist endeavors;
- ✓ Financial institutions that support the above;
- ✓ Infrastructure components (i.e., transportation, communications, utilities, or energy systems on which the above depend);

- ✓ Explosive magazine storage facilities (construction sites, quarries, etc.);
- ✓ Sports arenas, parks (theme and others);
- ✓ Schools, hospitals, shopping centers; and
- ✓ Venues for special events.

Identifying these potential targets is part of risk assessment.

Outward Warning Signs and Indicators

At the scene, initial responders need to be on the lookout for the following common warning signs indicating the presence of lethal agents from the five threat categories.

Remember, this is only a 'starter list'. There may be other hazards.

Biological Indicators

Biological incidents will present themselves in two ways. The first could be a community public health emergency, while the second could be a focused response to an incident, such as that involving a toxin.

The onset of some symptoms may take days to weeks, and typically there will be no characteristic signatures, because biological agents are usually odorless and colorless. Because of the delayed onset of symptoms, the number of victims and the areas affected may be greater due to the migration of infected individuals.

This geographical spread and time delay may make it more difficult for public health personnel to determine that the sickened people had a common exposure. Some effects may be very rapid (as short as 4 to 6 hours).

Exact indicators of a biological event may include:

- ✓ Unusual number of sick or dying people or animals;
- ✓ Dissemination of unscheduled and unusual sprays, especially outdoors or at night;
- ✓ Abandoned spray devices with no distinct odors.

You should consider calling local hospitals' infection control personnel to see if they have admitted additional casualties with similar symptoms.

Another useful contact is your health department's epidemiologist. Casualties may occur within minutes or hours, or may not occur until many days or weeks after an incident has occurred. The agent used determines the time during which the symptoms appear.

Nuclear Indicators

Short of an actual detonation or obvious accident involving radiological materials, there are a couple of ways to be certain that radiation is present:

- ✓ To observe the UN Dangerous Goods (DGR)/ Atomic Energy Licensing Board (AELB)/ International Atomic Energy Agency (IAEA) placards and labels.
- ✓ To use the monitoring devices that most fire department hazardous materials teams now carry routinely.

If the fire department does not have ready access to these instruments, the local or state office of emergency management should be able to provide them.

Find out about these organizations, what their response procedures are, and how to access them.

Incendiary Indicators

Multiple fires or multiple points of origin may indicate the use of accelerants such as gasoline, rags, or other incendiary devices.

Remains of incendiary device components, odors of accelerants, unusually heavy burning, or fire volume also are key indicators.

Chemical Indicators

Once released, a nerve agent's outward warning signs are easy to spot. Within minutes, the most significant sign will be rapid onset of similar symptoms in a large group of people.

Dermal exposure (clammy skin) and pinpoint pupils (miosis) are the best symptomatic indications of nerve agent use. Because nerve agents are so lethal, mass fatalities without other signs of trauma are common.

Other outward signs of nerve agent release include:

- ✓ Hazardous materials or lab equipment that is not relevant to the occupancy;
- ✓ Exposed individuals reporting unusual odors or tastes;
- ✓ Explosions dispersing liquids, mists, or gases;
- ✓ Explosions seeming only to destroy a package or bomb device;
- ✓ Unscheduled dissemination of an unusual spray;
- ✓ Abandoned spray devices;
- ✓ Numerous dead animals, fish, and birds;
- ✓ Absence of insect life in a warm climate;
- ✓ Mass casualties without obvious trauma;
- ✓ Distinct pattern of casualties and common symptoms; and civilian panic in potential target areas, i.e., government buildings, public assemblies, subway systems, etc.

Other chemical agents may have more diffuse warning signs. Large numbers of victims that are clustered in one area without obvious signs of trauma should be viewed as chemically-contaminated until proven otherwise.

Explosive Indicators

Signs of explosive incidents may be obvious, such as large scale damage to a building, or may be difficult to detect initially.

Blown-out windows and widely scattered debris also serve as indicators. Victims may exhibit effects of the blast, such as obvious shrapnel-induced trauma, appearance of shock-like symptoms, or damage to their eardrums.

Also, continue to maintain your situational awareness: there could be a secondary device targeting you and others.

Future Directions of Terrorism

Terrorists have shown an amazing capacity for change and adaptability, thus, you must be prepared for their future incident methods.

Cyber terrorism, an attack on our electronic communications systems in particular, is a very real possibility.

Other changes on the horizon may include usage of chimera biological agents (the use of gene splicing methods to combine the strengths of two separate bio agents into a new 'super bug'), attacks on financial networks and the destruction of physical infrastructure (bridges, water systems, etc.).

Recognize that what has worked for terrorists in the past, particularly the use of firearms and explosives, will probably continue to be used.

REMEMBER THIS!

A primary consideration is always to keep your personal safety and that of other responders in mind, then to help assure the preservation of evidence at the crime scene so as not to impede the investigation or prejudice ensuing litigation. The wisest course of action, although not the easiest, might be to delay entry and wait for the arrival of more highly trained personnel.

Responders in the habit of making quick responses will need to exercise a great deal of self-control in these situations, especially when human life is at stake. Specific steps that can be taken by the first responder at the awareness level are to isolate the scene, deny entry, notify additional resources, and recognize every key indicators of a potential terrorist incident.

FIRST AND FOREMOST, PROTECT YOURSELF!

Self-protection

Your self-protection is critical so that you can do your job effectively and not become a victim.

Your exercise of sound judgment and use of your personal protective equipment (PPE) according to design specifications are your initial steps to protecting yourself.

However, there are various protective countermeasures for the 7 common types of hazards.

Recognizing hazards and their physical effects

You could arrive at a potential terrorist incident and not really know what you're up against. Your first concern must be self-protection. You must recognize the various hazards that may be present at any kind of incident: biological, nuclear, incendiary, chemical, or explosive (B-NICE).

A single incident can present a variety of hazards and in most cases, exposure can be fatal. One commonly accepted classification identifies 7 types of harm you can encounter at an incident: **thermal, radiological, asphyxiative, chemical, etiological, mechanical and psychological**.

The acronym, **TRACEM-P**, is an easy way to remember them. Since each has different harmful effects, let's take a brief look at each.

Thermal

Thermal harm is the result of exposure to the extremes of **heat and cold**. Here we will examine only heat, but cold can be equally harmful. As you have learned elsewhere, heat travels by one of four methods: conduction, convection, radiation, and direct flame contact.

Radiological

Radiation, as used in this section, refers to **nuclear radiation**, not radiation as a type of heat transfer. There are three types of nuclear radiation that the first responder should be familiar with: **alpha, beta, and gamma**.

Alpha and beta radiation are found as particles, while gamma radiation is found in the form of rays. Alpha radiation is the least penetrating of the three, and is not considered dangerous unless alpha-contaminated particles enter the body. Once inside the body, alpha radiation will damage internal organs.

Beta radiation is more penetrating than alpha radiation. Beta-contaminated particles can damage skin tissue, and can harm internal organs if they enter the body.

Gamma radiation has great penetrating power. Gamma rays are high-energy, ionizing radiation that travels at the speed of light. They can cause skin burns, severely injure internal organs, and have long-term, physiological effects.

Asphyxiation

Asphyxiants interfere with or disrupt oxygen flow during normal breathing. There are generally two types of asphyxiants: simple and chemical.

Simple asphyxiants are inert gases that displace the oxygen necessary for breathing, and dilute the oxygen concentration below the level that is useful to the human body. Chemical asphyxiants are referred to as blood poisons, since they are compounds that interrupt the flow of oxygen in the blood or to the tissues. The asphyxiants prevent proper oxygen distribution and starve the body's cells of oxygen.

In all cases, the cells of the body are starved for oxygen. The asphyxiants prevent proper oxygen distribution. Examples of chemical asphyxiants include: **hydrogen cyanide (AC), cyanogen chloride CR), phosgene, carbon monoxide (CO), aniline, and hydrogen sulfide.**

Chemical

There are two broad types of chemicals used that can cause harm: toxic and corrosive materials. Both can exist as solids, liquids, or gases. Toxic materials produce harmful effects depending on the concentration of the materials and the length of exposure to them. An individual can have chronic or acute exposures to toxic materials. Nerve agents are examples of toxic materials.

Corrosive materials are liquids or solids causing visible destruction or irreversible alterations in human skin tissue at the site of contact. They may be liquids that have a severe corrosion rate on steel or aluminum. Sulfuric acid is an example of a corrosive material. Blister agents also behave like corrosives.

Of all the hazards that fall under the umbrella of hazardous materials, chemical hazards are probably most common. Yet, people are still injured and killed. Don't let your familiarity with this type of incident cause you to lower your preparedness.

Etiological

This type of harm involves exposure to a living microorganism, or its toxin, which causes, or may cause, human disease. Biological agents, such as anthrax or plague, are the most obvious examples of etiological agents. Again, the use of PPE will greatly enhance the responders' safety.

Consider also that depending on the biological agent, respiratory protection can be increased by an action as simple as wearing a properly fit-tested N-95 protective mask, although higher levels of protection may, in fact, be indicated for certain biological agents.

Mechanical

This most common type of harm causes trauma from contact with mechanical or physical hazards. One form of mechanical injury can result from an explosive device, in the form of shrapnel or antipersonnel materials, such as nails, contained in the explosion.

Advanced planning and forethought are required in order to avoid this type of harm. Other examples of mechanical harm include routine slip, trip, and fall hazards that are common to emergency response. It's easy to forget that these already account for a large number of responder injuries annually. Add the stress of responding to a terrorism incident and it seems obvious that care has to be taken not to 'cut corners' when it comes to safety.

Psychological

Sometimes we forget that a person can come away from an emergency response physically unhurt; yet still be injured. 'Psychological harm' refers to the emotional impact that a response to a terrorism incident can have on you. A terrorism incident may cause fatalities, numerous injuries--some quite grievous, disruption of essential community services, structural collapses, and so on.

Each of these may cause you or other responders to have psychological reactions. These reactions may be immediate or delayed. Concentration difficulty, sleep disorders, anxiety, emotional numbness, hyper vigilance — these may all be signs of a psychological reaction to a terrorism incident.

Time, Distance, and Shielding – The Keys to Self-Protection

Much of the traditional training in hazardous materials response builds upon these three methods, originally developed by the military, even though often the explicit link is not made, which are **time, distance, and shielding (TDS)**.

Time

You should spend the shortest amount of time possible in the hazard area and minimize the time of exposure to the hazard. Time is an ally when the hazard can be expected to become gradually less hazardous. Use time to protect yourself at a crime scene. Use techniques such as rapid entries to execute reconnaissance or rescue. Minimizing time spent in the affected area also will reduce the chance of contaminating the crime scene. Once the parameters of the incident are known, personnel not needed at the scene should be placed back in service or sent to a Staging Area.

Distance

Whenever you can distance yourself from the hazard, you should.

It should be an absolute rule always to maintain a safe distance from the hazard area or projected hazard area.

Remember that the greater the distance from the source of harm, the less the exposure.

Finally, it is generally advisable to be upwind and uphill of the source, if at all possible. Atmospheric conditions, such as wind, humidity, and precipitation all may impact the dispersion of an agent.

Shielding

As it makes good sense for you to let time and distance work in your favor, maintaining significant physical barriers between you and the hazard makes equally good sense.

Shielding can take various forms such as vehicles, buildings, walls, PPE, etc.

The use of PPE, including SCBA, will greatly increase your chances of a safe and successful response.

Experienced bomb technicians remind us that 'if you can see the bomb, the bomb can see you'. Shielding means more than just putting something big and heavy between you and 'it'.

You need to remember that no matter how much shielding is available and how safe you think it is, always take full advantage of time and distance. The 3 work best in tandem.

EVERY SITUATION IS DIFFERENT

When dealing with a potential terrorist incident, you are facing something unusual, something that, perhaps, you never have faced before. This could prove fatal, given the potential complexity of hazards and the specialized response skills needed. The situation may require atypical responses.

Before making any kind of response, you should evaluate the types of hazards involved and match to them the most appropriate response methods available to you.

TAKING CHARGE

Incident Command

The Incident Command System (ICS) is a standardized approach to the command, control and coordination of emergency response by providing a common hierarchy for responders from multiple agencies.

ICS is often thought to have begun in the fire services, with 1971 funding for the US Forest Service to design a system that will 'make a quantum jump in the capabilities of Southern California wild land fire protection agencies to effectively coordinate interagency action and to allocate suppression resources in dynamic, multiple-fire situations'. This became known as Firefighting Resources Organized for Potential Emergencies (FIRESCOPE).

However, Incident Command has clear antecedents in the US military's Command and Control (C2) system. Refined after the 1962 Cuban Missile Crisis, it became known as the Worldwide Military Command and Control System (WWMCCS).

C2 can be defined as the exercise of authority and direction by a properly

98

designated commanding officer over assigned and attached forces in the accomplishment of the mission.

In Malaysia, the National Security Council (NSC) is responsible for managing and coordinating emergency response and implementing security related policies in the country with a long history since its early inception in the late 1960's to improve public safety, national defence and preservation of public peace, supplies and services critical to the nation.

Command and control functions are performed through an arrangement of personnel, equipment, communications, facilities, and procedures employed by a commander in planning, directing, coordinating, and controlling forces and operations in the accomplishment of the mission.

Experience has shown that those incidents managed in a systematic way are the most successful at achieving the intended goals. Incident Command deals with the Incident Commander (IC) and staff making operational decisions, some strategic, others tactical in nature, and carefully allocating resources to implement them. You need to understand the role of the IC as the ultimate decision maker responsible for the outcome of the incident.

The ICS is a framework to manage the resources, personnel, apparatus, and equipment, used to mitigate the incident. Strategic decisions identify the overall approach to the incident, and operational decisions spell out the best use of those resources.

During routine emergencies, most firefighters follow a standard approach: performing size-up, choosing a strategy, implementing various tactics, and conducting ongoing evaluation.

Other methods have been developed to address new aspects related to non-routine situations. In these situations it is especially critical to know exactly what steps to take and the sequence in which they must occur because of the presence of hazards other than those traditionally encountered.

For example, during a bombing you may find it difficult to select appropriate course of action due to the incident's nature.

You may also feel extreme pressure to act. Regardless of the specific process used, responders go through a number of similar steps in dealing with their response.

The 5 common steps include conducting size-up, evaluating the situation, setting incident priorities, estimating potential incident circumstances and harm, and choosing strategic goals and tactical objectives.

Conducting Size-up

Size-up, the rapid mental evaluation of the factors that influence an incident, is the first step in determining a course of action. It begins even before the incident in the form of preplanning. The more information you have prior to the incident, the greater the chances of having a safe and successful response. Thus, what your communication centre can tell you as you respond to the call can provide you with important information.

Evaluating the Situation

Incident factors are dynamic and must be evaluated continually, so size-up continues as you arrive on the scene and make initial assessment.

You may have size-up indicators:

- ✓ Physical signs (unusual smoke colors or odors, etc.);
- ✓ Victim signs/symptoms indicating certain types of injuries; and
- ✓ Weather features, such as wind speed, humidity, etc.
- ✓ Incident situation refers to: the type, the cause, and the status of the incident.
- ✓ The type of incident: Whether it is one of the five types of incidents discussed: B-NICE (Biological, Nuclear, Incendiary, Chemical, and Explosives)
- ✓ The cause of the incident: Whether it is an accident, such as a system failure, or something intentional, such as a bombing.
- ✓ The incident status: Whether the incident is in a somewhat controlled state (static) or is still uncontrolled (dynamic or exposing).

Setting Incident Priorities

Incident priorities include life safety (this is the highest priority for the responders as well as the public);

Protecting critical systems (such as the infrastructure, including transportation, public services, and communication networks); and incident stabilization.

Estimating Potential Incident

Circumstances and Harm

Potential incident circumstances and harm includes a series of careful predictions based upon the assessment of incident situation and available information.

The responders estimate the probable course that the incident will take and the probable harm or damage that is likely to occur. For example, if faced with an explosion, you should be concerned about the possible presence of a secondary device that may cause harm to personnel or create additional property damage or structural collapse.

Choosing Strategic Goals and Tactical Objectives

Strategic goals are broad, general statements of the desired outcome. An example of a strategic goal would be 'to prevent loss of life for both civilians and responders'.

Tactical objectives are specific operations or functions to meet the goal. For example, to meet the strategic goal of preventing loss of life, you should 'isolate the hazard area and deny entry into that area'.

Tactics are the specific steps and actions taken by the assigned personnel to meet the determined objectives. For example, to accomplish the tactical objective of isolation, you could 'position apparatus in such a fashion as to block the area, and cordon off the area with banner tape'.

Notice that at each level there are more specifics involved. In the case of the tactical methods, using the apparatus and cordoning off the area are only two possible approaches.

Influence of Hazardous Materials

Hazardous materials curriculum for incident analysis process called GEDAPER was developed in the US by David M. Lesak, author of the 1998 book, 'Hazardous Materials: Strategies and Tactics' which is used by the US National Fire Academy as its model hazmat decision-making process.

GEDAPER provides first responders the needed processes for analyzing and handling a hazardous materials incident safely and prudently. This same tool can be helpful in dealing with the range of potential incidents.

GEDAPER

There are 7 steps to this process:

1. **G**athering information.
2. **E**stimating course and harm.
3. **D**etermining strategic goals.
4. **A**ssessing tactical options and resources.
5. **P**lanning and implementing actions.
6. **E**valuating.
7. **R**eviewing.

Gathering Information

You need to gather as much information about the incident as possible through observation, using the senses.

A first responder in personal protective equipment (PPE), including positive-pressure self-contained breathing apparatus (PP-SCBA), however, could only use sight and hearing.

Given the likelihood of the presence of hazardous materials at a terrorist incident, it would be in your best interest to observe from a distance, using only the senses of sight and hearing. The use of touch, taste, or smell could result in exposure.

Your awareness levels acquired from education, training, and experience will help you evaluate this information before going any further. Today, there are numerous information resources available in hard copy or electronic format. If you cannot access this information at the scene, contact those who can access it for you.

For instance when the term 'mass casualty incident' is used to describe an incident scene, you can relate to the situation automatically. The term triggers a mental assessment based on education, training, and experience. This is unavoidable. On top of this there are other layers. Perhaps many of technical information (data) provided by other sources, commonly including texts, computers, preplans, floor plans, etc.

There are other types of information that can assist you:

- ✓ Information received from your dispatcher, such as type of incident, incident location, number of reported casualties, etc., that could indicate a possible terrorist incident;
- ✓ Information obtained during your size-up, such as unusual signs and symptoms, presence of dead animals or people, unexplained odors, unusual metal debris, placards or labels, etc. (outward warning signs and detection clues);
- ✓ Environmental information, such as time of day or night, location (address, neighborhood, and occupancy), weather (temperature, wind direction, relative humidity), topography (lay of the land, hills, bodies of

water), and exposures (people, property, environment).

Regardless of the incident, the first step is to collect all the information possible as quickly as possible. Then, once you have made initial decisions, you need to continue to collect information and reassess it.

Estimating Course and Harm

This involves using the information gathered to make predictions and assess potential harm, concerning mainly, the damage assessment, hazard identification, vulnerability assessment, and risk determination.

Damage assessment involves figuring the damage that has already occurred. Hazard identification means determining what product is involved, where it is, what it can do, how much there is, etc.

Vulnerability assessment is figuring out whom and what is at risk, in other words, all persons and things the hazard may affect.

Risk determination involves estimating the probability that the situation might get worse before it is controlled.

Initially, strategic goals and tactical options should be based on the most likely situation outcome.

Determining Strategic Goals

Strategic goals are broad, general statement of intent. Always to be included in determining strategic goals are the incident priorities of life safety (responder and civilian), protection of critical systems (anything that is in place for the betterment of the community, such as public utilities and transportation, hospitals, etc.), and incident stabilization.

Assessing Tactical Options and

Resources

You need to select appropriate tactical objectives and methods. For instance, if the strategic goal is isolation, then the tactical objectives must include establishing perimeters and operational zones, denying entry into the 'hot zone', and removing the public and emergency personnel far from the 'hot zone'.

Perimeters and zones represent a safety factor, or buffer, against the hazards presented by the incident. The establishment of zones, or perimeters, is critical to protect both first responders and civilians. Denial of entry includes the use of physical barriers, such as tape, rope, barricades, etc.

Public protection involves establishing an area of safe refuge for those who are contaminated, thus reducing the chances of secondary contamination. It also involves assisting those individuals who are in harm's way to safety. Doing so will set the stage for decontamination and subsequent medical treatment.

All of these require the use of resources, including personnel and equipment. The level of effort required, coupled with the amount of resources available, will determine if the goals and objectives can be attained. If the resources are adequate, or if other assistance is available, then the next step, planning and implementing actions, becomes possible.

Withdrawal is an option where the situation is too dangerous or too large for intervention. The best course of action may be to evacuate the area, deny entry, and allow the incident to run its course.

Planning and Implementing Actions

The plan of action is a written document that consolidates all of the operational actions to be taken by various personnel in order to stabilize the incident. It is important for you to appreciate the purposes of the written plan. It helps pinpoint the exact actions planned.

Standard Operation Procedures/ Standard Operation Guidelines (SOPs/SOGs) are linked to the plan of action. They spell out the functions, roles, and responsibilities of personnel on the incident scene. They should be agreed on long before the incident, and the staff must be trained in implementing them.

Conducting drills and exercises shows how the SOPs/SOGs really should work. The plan of action should be tie up with references in accordance to the SOPs/SOGs.

Another important planning step is to create a 'site safety and health plan'. If the incident involves hazardous materials, which most terrorist incidents will, local legislations (i.e., OSHA) may require that you to create one.

A site safety and health plan is a series of checklists used to manage an incident and to assure the safety of all involved.

Like SOPs/SOGs, the checklists are developed before the incident and are implemented during the incident.

The site safety and health plan identifies the health and safety hazards faced at the incident scene. It further identifies appropriate PPE, decontamination considerations, emergency medical services (EMS) concerns, and similar safety issues.

When the incident involves chemical or biological hazards it assists in fulfilling employee rights.

Site safety and health plan helps to record specific actions and safety procedure used. It will assist in documenting whether the chosen plan of action and the specific procedures are followed. In addition, the site safety and health plan tracks activities and performances and assures that personnel safely perform those tasks for which they received appropriate training.

Someone trained only to the awareness level should not perform tasks specific to the operations or technician levels as it can be dangerous and even life threatening.

Included in the site safety and health plan are the location and the extent of zones, the nature of the hazards found on the scene, the types of PPE worn by personnel, and the type(s) of decontamination procedures which should be followed.

Your local or state hazardous materials responders should have examples of existing site safety and health plans that can be adjusted to fit a terrorist scenario.

Evaluating

The goal is to determine whether the plan of action is working as intended.

Evaluation will help identify possible errors and allow the responders to correct them.

You should be constantly evaluating and monitor all incident scenes, terrorist or not. If your plan is failing rapidly, you will need an alternate plan of action that can be implemented quickly and, depending on the available resources, used to solve the problem.

Reviewing

The review process involves revisiting and confirming the GEDAPER process.

Review occurs either when strategic goals are accomplished or when there is an extended response period and it is not wise to wait until the entire operation has concluded. If the entire process is managed effectively from the start, there should be no problems with the plan of action.

If the information gathered initially is thorough, comprehensive, and well managed, the estimate of course and harm should be accurate and the strategic goals and tactical objectives chosen also should be appropriate.

If problems are discovered with the plan, then the existing plan should be modified to reflect the appropriate changes, or a new plan should be developed to replace the flawed one.

The plan tells what should be, the evaluation tells what is not, and the review makes the corrections. Ongoing evaluation assures that the plan is working or alerts you that the plan is failing.

FIND SOLUTIONS, DON'T BECOME PART OF THE PROBLEM

While you may not be the IC, remember that the actions you take and the decisions you make early in the incident will have a dramatic effect on the outcome of the event.

One of the first concerns that you should address is your safety.

Dependent upon the situation you find upon your arrival, coupled with pre-arrival information such as the incident location and situation as dispatched, you will need to make early decisions that will affect the incident.

Always keep in mind the outward warning signs and detection clues mentioned.

On-scene considerations should be similar to your existing response guidelines dealing with hazardous materials.

While it would be easy to become overwhelmed, keep in mind the following key points:

> ✓ Your safety and that of your fellow personnel is paramount;

otherwise you can't possibly mitigate the incident. The initial steps of gaining control of the scene will greatly affect incident management.

✓ Simple procedures like staging apparatus uphill and upwind, performing isolation, and establishing perimeters, will help immensely. This may be all you can do prior to the arrival of additional resources, but don't minimize its importance.

✓ You need to be proactive, not reactive. Try to stay a few steps ahead of the current situation to be better prepared for what may occur next.

✓ You are only human and you can only do a limited number of tasks simultaneously. Although you may be overwhelmed initially, eventually your actions should overcome the seemingly chaotic situation and the incident will be under control.

Plan to be a part of the solution, not part of the problem, and don't hesitate to seek additional assistance.

When I was in the Aviation Security Academy many years ago, my AVSEC instructor always reminded our team that while it was good to be a hero, we should always be mindful that there are two kinds of heroes, a living hero and a dead hero.

At the end of the day, we should always strive to keep ourselves alive if we want to save lives.

PLANNING AHEAD

Activating Resources

It is vitally important that you realize the need for additional resources, and make the appropriate notifications to your communication centre.

Your locality and organization should have an emergency operations plan (EOP) in place to deal with incidents of such magnitude.

Occasionally, a natural or manmade disaster occurs which overwhelms resources and capabilities at the local level.

What is an Emergency Operations Plan?

An EOP is a document that:

✓ Assigns responsibility to organizations and individuals for carrying out specific actions at projected times and places in an emergency that exceeds the capability or routine responsibility of any one agency, e.g., the fire department;

✓ Sets forth lines of authority and organizational relationships, and shows how all actions will be coordinated;

✓ Describes how people, the environment, and property will be protected in emergencies and disasters;

✓ Identifies personnel, equipment, facilities, supplies, and other resources available—within the organization or by agreement with other organizations—for use during response and recovery operations; and

✓ Identifies steps to address mitigation concerns during response and recovery activities.

Who do you call?

You should always have an emergency call tree in hand, such as a break down list with categories of incidents and corresponding authorities in place:

Police
- Hold up/Robbery
- Bomb Threat
- Hijack/Kidnap
- Terrorist related activities/incidents
- Civil Unrest

Fire and Ambulance
- Fire/Explosion/Gas Leak
- Accidents
- Serious Injuries and Casualties

Civil Defense
- Flood, earthquake, etc.

Other useful contacts:
- Local municipal authorities
- Foreign consulates and embassies

ALWAYS KNOW YOUR ROLE

You must understand what happens during an incident, whether natural or manmade, your role in the notification process is the first link in the communications chain.

As soon as you suspect criminal activity or a potential act of terrorism, you should notify the appropriate authorities.

But mostly this does not extend beyond your dispatch or communications centre.

This will assist in activating available response resources, and increase the likelihood of success.

Useful links for further references

United Nations
www.un.org

Terrorism Research Council (USA)
www.terrorism.com

National Center for Biotechnology Information
(USA)
www.ncbi.nlm.nih.gov

Federal Emergency Management Agency (USA)
www.fema.gov

British Library (UK) Opac 97 Service
http://opac97.bl.uk

Global Terrorism Database (University of
Maryland, USA)
www.start.umd.edu/gtd

RAND Corporation
www.rand.org

Other books by the Author

Visit the Author's Page at:

www.amazon.com/author/khenhm